QED Write On

Imaginary
Creatures

Anne Faundez

© QED Publishing

QED

First published in the UK in 2005 by
QED Publishing
A Quarto Group company
226 City Road
London EC1V 2TT
www.qed-publishing.co.uk

A Catalogue record for this book is available from
the British Library.

ISBN 1 84538 182 3

Written by Anne Faundez
Designed by Alix Wood
Editor Hannah Ray
Illustrated by Nilesh Mistry

Series Consultant Anne Faundez
Publisher Steve Evans
Creative Director Louise Morley
Editorial Manager Jean Coppendale

Printed and bound in China

Contents

Imaginary creatures

The strange and wonderful creatures in this book are not real. They are characters from the great stories of the world.

They often live in magical places – in faraway forests, in the depths of the Earth, under the sea or near the Sun.

Dragon

European dragons are fierce and dangerous.
They are red or green and covered with scales.
They breathe fire through their nostrils and have
huge wings. They live underground, in caves
or under large boulders.

Oriental dragons are gentle
creatures that bring good luck.
They have a snake-like body
and can be any colour.

Griffin

This creature has the body of a lion, the wings and head of an eagle and the ears of a horse. Griffins are very strong. They pull the **chariots** of the Greek gods and goddesses.

8

Griffins live high up in the mountain peaks
of Asia and line their nests with gold.

Mermaid

A mermaid is half-woman, half-fish. Her home is at the bottom of the sea, but she likes to sit on the rocks and watch the ships sail past.

Mermaids are very vain. They spend a lot of time combing their long hair and looking into a mirror. They play the **lyre** and sing sweetly.

11

Phoenix

The phoenix is a large bird with gold, red and purple feathers.

Every 500 years, it flies to Egypt and builds a nest from sweet-smelling leaves and **spices**.

The sun's hot rays set the nest alight and the phoenix catches fire and dies.

But the next morning, the phoenix is alive again and flies away.

Scylla

Scylla is a monster with six heads, three rows of sharp teeth and twelve feet that end in sharp claws. Around her waist are the heads of dogs that never stop barking.

Scylla **guards** a narrow piece of sea between Italy and Sicily. She lies in wait, trying to catch sailors as they sail past.

15

Unicorn

Unicorns are the most beautiful imaginary creatures. They look like horses and are snowy white with long, flowing manes and tails.

Unicorns have blue eyes and horns in the middle of their foreheads. The horn is carved in a **spiral** shape and it can be white, gold, black or even rainbow-coloured.

Unicorns are shy and live in a faraway forest.

17

What do you think?

Which is your favourite imaginary creature?

Why have you never met an imaginary creature?

18

What colour
are unicorns?

Which do you think
is the scariest
imaginary creature?

What colour
feathers
does the
phoenix have?

Where do
dragons live?

What do griffins
use to line
their nests?

What instrument do
mermaids play?

21

Glossary

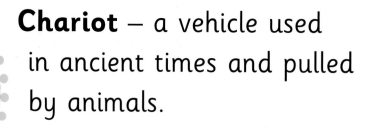

Chariot – a vehicle used in ancient times and pulled by animals.

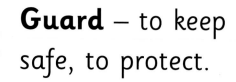

Guard – to keep safe, to protect.

Lyre – a musical instrument with strings.

Spices – parts of a plant, such as the leaves and seeds, that smell strongly when dried.

Spiral – a line that goes round and round in circles and gets larger and larger.

Index

Parents' and teachers' notes

- Look at the cover of the book together. What might the book be about? Talk about the picture that is on the cover. Read the title of the book. Does your child know what the word 'imaginary' means?
- Point out the author's name. Explain to your child that the 'author' is the person who has written the book.
- Emphasize that the creatures discussed in this book are not real. They exist in stories and in people's imagination.
- Explain that the book gives information about the creatures, and is therefore a non-fiction book, even though the creatures themselves are not real.
- Explain that a non-fiction book can be dipped into, and does not have to be read from beginning to end. Choose a page at random, and read it together.
- Tell your child that a non-fiction book usually has a contents page, a glossary and an index. Locate each of these in the book and explain their purpose. Use the contents page to find the pages on the phoenix.
- Explain that the phoenix is an imaginary creature that was created by the ancient Egyptians many thousands of years ago. The phoenix also appears in stories from China, Ancient Greece and many other countries.
- Look at the pages on Scylla. Explain that Scylla was a monster created by Homer, a storyteller from ancient Greek times who lived thousands of years ago. In his story, 'The Odyssey', the hero Odysseus and his crew had to sail past Scylla. She managed to catch some of his sailors, but Odysseus was unharmed.
- Can you and your child think of any stories that feature dragons?
- Challenge your child to paint a dragon breathing fire.
- Act out a conversation between a European dragon and an Oriental dragon. What might they say to each other? What would their voices sound like?
- Together, create your own imaginary creature. What will it look like? What colours will it be? What will it be called? Will it be scary or friendly? Where will your imaginary creature live? Encourage your child to paint a picture of his or her imaginary creature.
- Together, write a few sentences to describe your child's imaginary creature.
- Make up a story about your creature. Help your child to write down the story, and then encourage him or her to add some illustrations.